The Power
Of Simplicity

Choosing
to live your life on purpose

Patty Kreamer

Janet,
Here's) to
The POWER! Warmly,

Paty Kreamer

First Edition

Publish Connect * Pittsburgh * PA

The Power of Simplicity
Choosing to live your life on purpose

Patty Kreamer

Published by:
Publish Connect
Pittsburgh, PA

Printed in the United States of America

ISBN: 0-9745135-2-0 (Paperback)

Library of Congress Cataloging-in-Publication Data

Kreamer, Patty.
The Power of Simplicity: Choosing to live your life on purpose
Library of Congress Control Number: 2004090360

To my sisters Diane and Kathy. As the saying goes, there is nothing in the world like a sister. I cherish you both.

TABLE OF CONTENTS

Foreword

I never think much about simplicity…I usually don't have the extra time. Instead, I have spent the last 30 years of my life complicating it. It now takes extra time every day just to handle these complications–a vicious cycle and one I found hard to break.

Until I met Patty Kreamer. I knew there was something different about her the first time we were introduced. She is open and focused and very clear in her words and actions. When I found out that she was a professional organizer, I was intimidated. I think of myself as an amateur disorganizer. I use my creative endeavors such as writing as an excuse. I knew there was a better way, but no one had the patience to show me the light.

I did some editing on Patty's first book, *…But I Might Need It Someday*, and I read a number of the suggestions over and over–not because they were poorly written, but because they made such sense! I actually implemented some of them. And it was good. My clutter is still not good, but there is less of it. It is liberating.

Now, Patty Kreamer is taking her ideas to a new level. She is sharing the power that is unleashed by making clear and simple life choices. Great advice, even for a complex woman such as me. Each time I read a part of this book, I make a new plan to make a change that will better my life. Some of us cannot follow the whole program, but all of us can benefit from the advice. This will become one of the major goals of my life: simplify, simplify, simplify.

I recommend several readings of this book; don't overwhelm yourself trying to do it all at one time. But a change in the direction of simplicity will liberate your soul. Thank you, Patty!

Suzanne Caplan

Author and National
Business Speaker

ACKNOWLEDGEMENTS

A sincere thanks to:

Suzanne Caplan. You suddenly took me under your wing and shared your time, talent, and expertise with me. You've helped me not only through your words, but also your actions. I don't know what I did to deserve you in my life, but I am grateful for you and your gifts. You wear more hats than anyone I know...and you wear them all well. Thank you.

Jennifer McGuiggan. I wrote the words, you made them sound better. Thank you for your exceptional style.

And a special thank you to the following people for dedicating your precious time to read this book and offering valuable feedback. Your insight helped in the final stretch more than you know.

> Shirley Englert
> Leslie McKee
> Barry Izcak
> Susan Owens
> Bonnie Budzowski
> Al Arends
> Terri Sokoloff
> Carol Briney
> Vickie Delaquilla
> Donna Rossa

The Power
Of Simplicity

INTRODUCTION

Simply Speaking...

...life is simple. Period.

If everybody had that attitude, not only would I be surprised, but I could stop writing right now!

The issue is that as human beings, we tend to allow life to be difficult. Unfortunately, we are not alien creatures that would be satisfied with just the basics of survival: air, water, food, and shelter.

Technically, we could survive with just the bare minimum. After all, it was not too long ago when electricity, television, telephones, running water, and many of today's luxuries were non-existent. Nonetheless, it is the choices we make that allow *more* than is necessary to enter the picture. This abundance then requires continual feeding in order to maintain that lifestyle. It becomes a never-ending cycle.

Even today, there are folks that can and do live with few modern creature comforts. They have no TV (sit down and put your head between your knees if you can't breath), no car (are you serious?), no computer (holy cow!), or no microwave oven (dear Lord, what are these people thinking?).

On the other end of the spectrum, there are those that keep piling it on, trying to keep up with the Joneses (or they are the Joneses), getting involved in any activity despite the time commitment, and buying any new gadget regardless of the consequences.

What makes these people different? It all boils down to CHOICE. Believe it or not, you have a choice in (almost) EVERYTHING you do in life. You just have to stop long enough to realize that. (You'll always have to pay taxes and you're going to die, so those don't count.)

CHOICE

Contemplate
Having
Only
If
Considered
Essential

You have probably visited someone's home that had no clutter, where everything was in its place, and you could eat off the floor. If you happen to live a less than simplified life, you may ask yourself, how (or why) do they live like this? The answer is that they probably made the conscious choice to live that way.

Even though life is simple, simplicity is difficult. Sound like an oxymoron? Well, it is!

The word simplicity itself makes you think that it would be easy to attain. But the concept of simplicity should not be confused with "little effort." Although simplicity is not easy to achieve, the end result makes the journey worthwhile.

> ## Simplicity is a lifestyle, not an event.

But wait! How can you even consider simplifying your life with the escalating pace that we are expected to keep up with each day? Everywhere you look, you instantly have access to any item that you want. You are reminded of the time, money, and freedom that you will sacrifice if you don't move and accumulate at warp speed. There's:

- ❏ Fast food
- ❏ High-speed Internet
- ❏ Instant messaging
- ❏ Five minute oil changes
- ❏ Eyeglasses in an hour
- ❏ Rapid refund
- ❏ Instant rebates
- ❏ Buy now
- ❏ Instant credit
- ❏ Two years same as cash
- ❏ HURRY! HURRY! HURRY!

Pittsburgh, PA radio station KDKA AM 1020 has a slogan that says, "If you are reading about it, it's history; if you are hearing about it, it's news." This sentence captures the essence of how quickly time races by.

By getting caught up in all of this, you find that there are natural consequences of living and accumulating without a purpose and without forethought. "Stuff" begins to take over your life, and, before you know it, you need a bigger, higher maintenance home to store it all. You gather without thinking about whether there is a place in your life for the new stuff. Family takes a backseat. Work and outside activities consume you day and night. Sure, technology *saves* you time, but you just fill it with more tasks.

Most people will agree that adding more and more to their lives is stressful. On the flip side, the benefits of voluntarily simplifying your life are many. A simplified life contains only what matters most. You will learn to live without the (literal) excess baggage that you have been toting around for years. More important, you will discover that you don't miss the chaos…at all.

Do you ever wonder what it might be like:

- To have some time to do what you *want* to do and not what you *have* to do?
- To sit down and relax for an hour without feeling guilty because you should be doing something else?
- To arrive fresh and early for an appointment instead of the usual 15-20 minutes late, spewing out apologies and excuses for your tardiness?
- To be able to find something the minute you need it and not weeks later after you've already gone out and bought a replacement?
- To welcome unexpected company any time of the day without being embarrassed?
- To enjoy the activities that you have planned because they stand out rather than blend in with the fast pace of the day?

With the POWER OF SIMPLICITY, you can achieve any and all of the above. The POWER can be so strong that once you get a taste of it, you'll wonder how you ever led the life of a fast-paced, jam-packed, never-stopping, always-running, crazed individual.

If this way of life appeals to you and you are READY to wander away from the rushing rat race that you now live in, you will find this book full of thought-provoking gems and commonsense nuggets to put you on the path to simplicity.

Finally, here is a book that spells out how to *achieve* what you have been seeking for years—happy, stress-free, simple living.

Prepare to UNLEASH THE POWER OF SIMPLICITY and live your life on purpose!

Here's to simplifying your life,

Patty

P.S. I recommend that you read this book several times with your favorite color highlighter in hand!

A day in the life of simplicity

You wake up each morning at the same scheduled time. You feel refreshed because you had the exact amount of sleep that you require to function at your best. As you approach your closet, you have no problem choosing your outfit for the day. The selection does not overwhelm you with six shades of blue for which you can never seem to find the matching shoes.

During your shower, you enjoy the feeling of the hot water washing over you rather than rushing through with a speed rinse so you can make up for running late after sleeping in. Total shower and prep time: 30 minutes, and that includes a few extra minutes to dawdle in the shower.

Your path to the kitchen is free of debris since stuff no longer rules your life. You prepare a quick and healthy breakfast for you and the family. Everyone joins the breakfast table well rested and ready for the day.

After taking the roast out the night before, you pop it into the crock-pot so it will be ready when you get home from work. Your son will prepare a salad when he gets home from school and your daughter will take care of the starch.

The only activities planned this morning are school and work; the swim team practices were too much every morning, so you decided as a family to try a new activity that didn't disrupt everyone's routine. Your daughter was disappointed at first, but realized that her days were wearing thinner as well and now enjoys being a part of the debate team instead. The tradeoff was worthwhile.

You arrive at the office ten minutes early in a great mood.

As you go through your day, you check your calendar to see what you have scheduled. Before you left yesterday, you made sure that you had planned 70-80 percent of your day in your day planner, leaving room for emergencies and interruptions. You notice that since you have been doing this, you don't feel so overwhelmed throughout the day. You know what needs to be done and by the end of the day, you are able to complete exactly what you planned.

Since spending the time to organize your office, you know where things are and have no trouble retrieving your files from your new system.

At the end of the day, you leave at quitting time. You used to stay two extra hours, but that is no longer necessary since you are in control of your time.

When you arrive home, you can smell the roast wafting through the house. The table has been set and the meal is ready to be served. The family sits down to a homemade meal and everyone takes turns talking about his or her day. You linger around the table for an extra twenty minutes enjoying each other's company.

Homework is completed and the family chooses their activity for the night: television, a game, a discussion, or maybe a drive.

At the same time as last night, everyone goes to bed and the same routine begins again. It doesn't occur to you to be bored. You are in touch with what you want and are so appreciative for having it on a daily basis.

Gone are the stress, headaches, hustle and bustle, and frustrations. Your days are filled with joy, love, clarity, and happiness.

Imagine that....

CHAPTER 1

Imagine the possibilities of simplicity

Ah, to live the life of the Cleavers....

Remember the television show *Leave it to Beaver*? You may remember the Cleavers or perhaps you've seen the reruns. Here's how the show went: Parents June and Ward Cleaver started their day having breakfast with their children, Wally and the Beaver. Dad went to work, Wally and the Beaver went to school, and Mom stayed home and tended to the house and family. Later, they all came home to enjoy a family dinner, spent the evening together doing homework and talking about their day, and then they were off to bed.

Life was so simple then. Of course, they had their ups and downs; otherwise it would have been a one-episode series! But the family was always the number one priority and life wasn't very complicated.

The Cleavers had no computer, no video games, no personal digital assistants (PDAs), no Internet, no microwave oven, no cell phone (gasp!), no email, no 24/7 connectivity to the world.

Wouldn't it be great if life were that simple again? You can't go back technologically, but you can make choices about what and how much you allow into your life.

If your life is similar to the Cleavers', you deserve my sincere congratulations. But if you are among the many people constantly trying to keep their head above water and you think that the lifestyle of the Cleavers is not possible to attain, I urge you to reassess your beliefs.

> "If you think you can or
> think you can't, you're right."
>
> - Henry Ford

If you listen to other people (maybe even yourself), and pay close attention, you can hear the obvious lack of simplicity in their lives through everyday chatter. You hear it on the telephone, in person, through email, at the water cooler, and just about anywhere that people gather.

You'll hear such things as:

- ❑ I am *so* busy.
- ❑ I *never* have any time for myself.
- ❑ I am *always* running late.
- ❑ I *never* make dinner…I make reservations.

❏   I can't remember the last time my family ate together....
❏   I didn't have a chance to...
❏   I am *always* so tired.
❏   I wish I had time to...
❏   My office is *so* messy I can't get any work done.
❏   My house is a disaster area.
❏   I never have company...it's too embarrassing!
❏   I never stop running all day long, but I get so little done.
❏   Our family *never* gets together...we're all so busy.

It is sad to note that people are so busy they don't even take the time for common courtesies or simple manners anymore. "Please" and "thank you" are noticed more now because they are so rare. It used to be that you noticed when you did NOT hear these phrases.

Wouldn't it be great to eliminate any and all of the stressors listed above from *your* life? You can. You can tame the tornado that you call your life by simply choosing to make some changes, which is why you chose to read this book. Just remember, you will have a better chance of achieving simplicity if you are **READY** to do so.

> # To make changes, you must first recognize the need for change.

WHAT IS SIMPLICITY?

I don't equate simplicity with minimalism. The word minimalism carries a negative connotation, as if you have to live on just the bare necessities of life. This is *not* what most people are seeking. People want quality over quantity. This entails having whatever you like in your life as long as what you have matters. Simplicity can mean different things to different people.

> I believe that simplicity is having only what you truly need to be happy.

Simplicity is a choice. A decision. The bottom line is that only *you* are responsible for what you bring into your life. Period.

The term "voluntary simplicity" is sometimes used to label what I'm describing. This trend is emerging as people find themselves frustrated, forgetting to live, and running through each day without any thought. They want to learn how to live a fuller life with less. They want to stop running and start *living*.

One of my friends knows a man who once said, "Sometimes I like to step off the world and let it make a few rotations without me." Believe it or not, the world will *not* come to an abrupt halt just because you choose to simplify your life and take a break from the madness.

> By simplifying your life, you can substantially improve your quality of life.

Our culture encourages us to have everything that we WANT, and I doubt that we would want it any other way. However, this allows us to accumulate things swiftly without taking the time to think about whether we have room in our lives to accommodate them. People rarely, if ever, ask themselves WHY they want something. They just keep piling it on with no regard to the consequences that will eventually manifest.

If you happen to be a marketing specialist, I apologize for what you are about to read. (I have a Bachelor of Science degree in marketing from Indiana University of Pennsylvania, so while I fully appreciate the marketing profession, I feel it is my duty to share some secrets with my readers.)

When you go into a store to buy one or two items, it is not by accident that you leave with 15 to 20 things that you hadn't planned to purchase. Marketing experts count on you to buy on *impulse*, and just in case you don't do that naturally, they set up the store to be sure that you will.

I received *The Retailers Catalog* in the mail and one of the first items on the inside cover is an Impulse Table (they really call it that!) that you see when you first walk into a store or at the end of the aisles. It's a setup!

You are a victim before you even walk through the doors!

All sorts of "invisible" details are well thought out: the colors and patterns of the floor, the piped-in music, the placement of the racks, the displays at the end of the aisles, the temperature and scents of the store, and the colors of the displays, the products, and their packaging. Retailers study what makes people buy and set up their stores accordingly.

Don't believe it? Go to your local mall or even your grocery store and focus on some or all of these characteristics. You will see the trap being laid out before you as you've never noticed before.

One of the best examples of marketing to impulse is cereal. The next time you are at the grocery store, notice the eyes of the cartoon characters on the cereal boxes. They are all looking down. Accident? Not likely. This is done intentionally because children are short. The characters make eye contact with the kids and they connect. The characters do the marketing to the kids, who in turn market the product to you by asking for it.

Another great example is cereal's natural partner – milk. Do you really think that milk is at the back of the grocery store by mistake? Think again. Milk is a frequently replaced staple that is often intended to be the sole purchase of a shopping trip. By making you walk to the very back of the store (usually to the furthest corner from the entrance), your impulse buying can—and will—kick into high gear.

It is up to you as a consumer to process each potential purchase through a more developed **filter**. This filter will not only work on physical clutter, but on mental, emotional, and time clutter as well.

We will start by focusing on the "NEED vs. WANT" filter to demonstrate how it can be used in many areas of your life.

REVIEW / EXERCISE

I often say the following:

- ❑ I am *so* busy.
- ❑ I *never* have any time for myself.
- ❑ I am *always* running late.
- ❑ I *never* make dinner…I make reservations.
- ❑ I can't remember the last time my family ate together.
- ❑ I didn't have a chance to…
- ❑ I am *always* so tired.
- ❑ I wish I had time to…
- ❑ My office is *so* messy I can't get any work done.
- ❑ My house is a disaster area.
- ❑ I never have company…it's too embarrassing!
- ❑ I never stop running all day long, but I get so little done.
- ❑ Our family *never* gets together…we're all so busy.

Do you notice when someone is courteous? List some examples.

_____

_____

Are you ready for voluntary simplicity? If so, why?

_____

_____

Have you ever noticed the marketing set-up in stores? Give examples.

_____

_____

NOTES

_____

_____

_____

CHAPTER 2

Tackling the physical side of simplicity

Stress is a major contributing factor to poor health. Physical clutter adds to that stress, often without your knowledge, because clutter is what you no longer see. You walk around the piles of magazines, and you really don't see them. But I can guarantee that your head and stomach "feel" them; you get a wave of guilt from ignoring the problem. Perhaps you fear throwing things away because you might miss something.

A way to test this stress theory is to remove the clutter and feel the difference. If you are having a difficult time seeing the clutter in question, take a look around your space through a stranger's eyes, as if company were coming. This is a surefire way to bring to light all of the items that you have been ignoring for a long time.

Clutter has no conscience. It interacts with all of the other types of clutter to make your life a vicious cycle. In other words, clutter produces clutter. Here's how it works: Physical clutter produces mental clutter, mental clutter produces time clutter, time clutter produces emotional clutter, and the circle never ends.

If you have a ton of stuff (physical clutter) lying around, it causes stress (mental clutter). As you angrily search for something, you cause yourself to be late and hurried to your next appointment (time clutter). On the way to your appointment, you internally curse yourself for the way things are in your life and you begin to cry (emotional clutter). To make yourself feel better, you promise to go out and buy a new pair of shoes later on (more physical clutter!).

CLUTTER CAN:

❑   Make you sick
❑   Make you feel tired
❑   Affect your body weight
❑   Keep you living in the past
❑   Cause or worsen depression
❑   Make you put your life on hold
❑   Induce a feeling of shame and guilt
❑   Be the main cause of procrastination
❑   Add unnecessary confusion in your life
❑   Make you feel that there is no alternative
❑   Affect how people treat and/or respect you
❑   Cause disharmony among family, friends, or coworkers

> # Clutter is nothing more than unmade decisions.

The existence of physical clutter should come as no surprise since we live in such a prosperous time. The problem is that we want everything and we want it NOW. Since we live in a climate of instant gratification, we can have most things whenever we want them. But we do not need most of what we have in our lives. The "stuff" accumulates and is never given a proper home. Thus, clutter is born.

If you are able to get your physical clutter under control, the mental clutter is likely to follow without much effort, since one causes the other. For example, if you go into a cluttered room or office, you immediately tense up. If you go into that same room or office after you have decluttered it, you feel liberated. Your time becomes yours again, your priorities fall back into place, and best of all, your health may improve.

> ## Control your clutter
> ## before it controls you!

The "NEED vs. WANT" Filter

Since the first step to simplicity is getting your "stuff" under control, let's examine how to apply the "NEED vs. WANT" filter to physical clutter.

Picture yourself shopping in your favorite store. As you traverse the aisles, you can almost see the marketing gurus standing in the wings watching you on the monitor as you walk right into their sneaky wallet-emptying traps.

Listen closely and you can almost hear them giggling as you put that unnecessary item into your cart. STOP RIGHT THERE! This is where you can throw a monkey wrench into their plan. You have to muster up the courage to fight the battle and ask yourself a serious question:

Do I NEED or WANT this item?

If your answer is…

I **NEED** this item, ask yourself:

Where will this live when I get it back to my home or office?

If there is no room for it, the second question to ask is:

What will I get rid of in order to make room?

If your answer is…

I **WANT** this item, ask yourself:

Can I live without this item?

Can I wait a week to make the purchase?

Do I really want to spend my money on this item?

You can significantly change your shopping perspective and behavior by asking yourself if you need or want things. Instead of automatically adding something to your cart, you will first run it through the above series of filters to make sure it "fits" into your life.

If you are able to postpone any purchase by a week, you will considerably reduce the number of purchases you make. Think of the money you'll save! You will forget about 90 percent of the items that you postpone, proving that these were merely impulse items. Here's my definition of impulse:

IMPULSE

I
Must
Purchase
Until
Logic
Surpasses
Emotion

If you are at the mall and see something that you just *have* to have, *and* it's on sale, make a mental note of what you can donate to make room for the new item AS SOON AS YOU GET HOME!

For example, our kitchen is eight feet by eight feet, so there's not much room for extras. If I am shopping and decide to buy a new small appliance, I have to seriously think about where it will live. For this, I use the ONE IN – ONE OUT rule.

ONE IN – ONE OUT

If you have run an item through the "NEED vs. WANT" filter and decided that you do need it and there is room, you need to employ the next step towards simplicity: the **ONE IN – ONE OUT rule.**

This is really simple: When you buy something new, get rid of something old. Buy a new pair of shoes, throw away or donate an old pair. (I can just see you wincing in pain at the thought of getting rid of a pair of shoes, but you can do it—I know you can! Try throwing away those shoes that have the toe pointing upward from old age and dryness. Only an elf would be able to wear them, so it's safe to say you can pitch them.) Even if you have room for the new pair, getting rid of an old pair is a great way to avoid buildup and future clutter. It is part of the ebb and flow of life.

If you want to make really quick progress in decluttering your life, instead of getting rid of one item to make room for the new, get rid of two, three, or four! So you can do one in – one out, – two out, – three out, and so on. Obviously the higher the OUT number, the faster you will see results.

ONE OUT – ONE IN

If you have ever experienced the phenomenon that clothes shrink when they live in a closet for a while (who knew?), try working in reverse by using the ONE OUT – ONE IN rule. For example, when you change your wardrobe in the spring and fall, toss out or donate the items you no longer wear or want (OUT). Then determine what is missing—for instance, you need a new white blouse or black slacks—and go shopping to fill those gaps (IN).

We have small closets in our home (as you may have guessed), so space is limited. This not only prevents us from having more stuff than we NEED (by choice), it also helps us save money.

The ONE IN – ONE OUT and the ONE OUT – ONE IN rules can apply to anything that you bring into your life, not just clothes. It works for furniture, linens, a new hobby, food, shoes, books, computer equipment, office supplies, activities, and even a new friendship.

Parents, this is a fabulous rule to teach your children. What a great gift to give them, teaching them to be generous, simplified, and organized all at the same time.

How do I conquer the IMPULSE?

If you naturally respond to advertising and succumb to impulse, here's what you need to do.

STOP

- ❏ Shopping unnecessarily
- ❏ Reading advertisements
- ❏ Watching so much TV
- ❏ Receiving junk mail
- ❏ Opening junk mail
- ❏ Reading catalogs
- ❏ Keeping catalogs
- ❏ Receiving junk email
- ❏ Opening junk email
- ❏ Surfing the Internet
- ❏ Attending flea markets
- ❏ Attending garage sales
- ❏ Attending yard sales (get the picture?)

AND START

- ❏ Understanding what makes you buy
- ❏ Canceling junk mail (see box)
- ❏ Canceling junk email (see box)
- ❏ Canceling telemarketers (see box)
- ❏ Canceling catalogs
- ❏ Canceling the newspaper
- ❏ Taping TV shows - fast-forwarding through ads
- ❏ Recognizing what impulse feels like
- ❏ Exercising willpower and restraint
- ❏ Setting up a table to *SELL* at flea markets
- ❏ *Having* garage sales
- ❏ *Having* yard sales

Remove yourself from junk mail lists

Visit The Direct Marketing Association's website at www.the-dma.org and click on

- ❏ For Consumers
- ❏ Remove my name from marketing lists
- ❏ Mailing Lists
- ❏ Telephone Lists
- ❏ Email Lists

In order to make your life simpler, you need to stop exposing yourself to what complicates it. Achieve this by changing your environment to include less of the stimuli that contribute to your impulses. This aids in diminishing the temptation to buy things that you don't need in your life.

I know, I know…if you throw the catalogs away, you are afraid you will miss something. This is a common fear for which catalog companies pray. You should be more afraid that you'll buy something! Here's the deal: If you don't see it, you don't know you missed it. There are so many things that get by us on a daily basis that we don't even know about. You can't know it all, and that should comfort you, not panic you.

If it makes you feel any better, know that a *single* daily edition of *The New York Times* contains more information than a person in the early 1800's learned in their *lifetime*. In other words, you don't have to, and can't, know it all. You are bombarded on a daily basis with much more information than you can handle. Take steps to minimize the information in your life.

According to *Leadership* magazine, one researcher noted that the average desk-worker has 36 hours worth of work on the desk, and spends three hours a week just sorting through it.

When you finally get out from under the clutter, chaos, and disorder, you will likely never want to go back to that way of life again. However, the physical side of simplicity is only one part of the bigger picture. If you want to change the physical clutter side of your life, you will need to work on the mental and emotional part, which is based on your beliefs.

Your behavior is directly related to your beliefs. Therefore, it makes sense that if you change your beliefs, your behavior will follow. Maybe you have never thought about your beliefs or attitudes and where they come from. At the very least, it's interesting to look a little deeper and discover WHY you do what you do. Since your beliefs drive your behaviors, this process is a worthwhile time investment to understand what steers you through life.

If you really want to simplify your life, you MUST be willing to change your beliefs; your behavior will follow.

For example, if you *believe* that you need to have more things, then you will never change your *behavior* of shopping to obtain them. If, on the other hand, you start to question WHY you *believe* you need to bring things into your life, you will begin to see changes.

In my book *...But I Might Need It Someday! How to organize your life and WIN the clutter battle once and for all*, I thoroughly examine beliefs, behaviors, and tools from a clutter and organizing standpoint. If you need help in clarifying your beliefs about your physical possessions, you might want to include this book on your reading list. The book is available at www.ByeByeClutter.com.

In order to achieve simplicity, you need to examine the physical possessions that may contribute to your busy, crammed, and hurried lifestyle. Remember, it didn't take you a day to complicate your life, so you won't be able to simplify it in one day either. Simplifying your life is a process, not an event. This process may not be easy, but the payoff is phenomenal!

REVIEW / EXERCISE

Do I NEED or WANT this item?

If I **NEED** this item, ask:

Where will this live when I get it back to my home or office?

If there is no room for it, the second question to ask is:

What will I get rid of in order to make room?

If I **WANT** this item, ask:

Can I live without this item?

Can I wait a week to make the purchase?

Do I really want to spend my money on this item?

What have you purchased recently that the ONE IN – ONE OUT rule could apply to?

☐ _____
☐ _____
☐ _____
☐ _____

Remove yourself from junk mail lists

Visit The Direct Marketing Association's website at
www.the-dma.org then
Click on "For Consumers" tab.
Click on "Remove my name from marketing lists."
Click on "Mailing Lists, Telephone Lists, or Email Lists."

CHAPTER 3

Confronting the
emotional side of simplicity

It's time to change your soundtrack.

From a very young age, many children are taught that they
should not waste, that they should use and keep everything
they have. This Depression-era mentality instills a sense of
guilt that results in clutter accumulation because we feel that
we must keep, keep, keep everything! It's like a soundtrack
playing in your head every time you try to release something
from your life, saying, "YOU MUST NOT BE WASTEFUL!
YOU MUST NOT BE WASTEFUL!"

Letting go seems like an unacceptable option because you have been taught just the opposite all of your life. But you *can* do it.

Rather than playing the same soundtrack over and over again, why not create a new tape with a new dialog? When the old soundtrack tells you not to waste anything, ask yourself which is more valuable:

o The things that you have accumulated and trip over daily, causing stress beyond your level of tolerance;

OR

o The space and peace of mind that you will reclaim by eliminating these same items?

If you usually make decisions from an emotional standpoint, you may find the above question hard to answer. However, using logic will make the second choice obvious. Emotion might bring guilt, fear, stress, and several other *feelings* into play. Logic, however, dismisses feelings and goes to the *thinking* side of decision-making.

> # Logic plays a
> # huge role in simplicity.

QUESTION: How do I begin to eliminate my guilt, stress, and fear in order to achieve to simplicity?

ANSWER: Give yourself permission.

Letting go is tough. It begins by granting yourself permission to do so. Think of it as getting back to square one by letting go of the things that you have held onto for so long out of guilt, duty, or obligation. Your reward is a healthier, happier, and less stressful life. Once you reach square one, you must be discriminating about what you allow into your life.

> ## The person that can make you feel most guilty is YOU!

QUESTION: How do you give yourself permission to go against what you have been taught your whole life?

ANSWER: Learn how you think differently.

> ## Looking at your stuff, it's easier to *feel* what it means to you than it is to *think* about what it is doing to you.

Typically, when you make a decision, you base it on one of two things: emotion or logic. Naturally, if you are an emotional or sentimental person, you probably tend to keep items for reasons that *seem* logical to you. But if you deeply examine those reasons, you can break them down to see that your heart plays a bigger part than your head.

The key words here are **feel** and **think**. Understand that you don't have to remove all feeling from your life. You just need to examine where your thoughts stem from so that you can arm yourself with a more practical point of view.

Here are some examples of Logical vs. Emotional thinking.

EMOTIONAL: "Who cares about the lost space? I could never throw away my college papers."

LOGICAL: "Those college papers are from 18 years ago. Sure, I was brilliant when I wrote them. (Man, I was good!) But even though I put a lot of effort into them, I don't remember writing them and they really are outdated. I haven't looked at them since graduation, so they can't be that important to me. In fact, I didn't even know they were here until we decided to move. How important can they be?"

EMOTIONAL: "If I donate my 'smaller' clothes, I may not have enough incentive to get back into them."

LOGICAL: "If I get rid of my 'smaller' clothes and lose the weight that I want to lose, that will give me the opportunity to get a whole NEW wardrobe as a reward and get rid of my 'larger' clothes!"

EMOTIONAL: "I have to keep these gas, electric, and cable bills because I might need them someday."

LOGICAL: "I have rarely referred back to these bills, and the utility companies said that if I need a copy of any bill in the future, I can get them by mail, email, or online. I'll let the utility company store them for me, knowing that if I need a copy, I can get one in a timely manner. That's good enough for me."

EMOTIONAL: "I am so sentimental that I couldn't bare to part with my grandmother's broken rocking chair."

LOGICAL: "I remember Grandma sitting in that rocking chair. It brings back great memories, but I don't need the chair cluttering up my home to remember her. The chair is not the memory; the memory is the memory. Perhaps a photo of the chair would be nice to look at from time to time to jog my memory, but I don't need the chair itself. This is the same concept as looking at pictures from past vacations and remembering the fun."

Can you see the difference in the thought process? If simplifying your life is important, you **can** rewrite the soundtrack that constantly runs in your head telling you to keep everything. It sounds as it does now because that is what you were taught from a young age. Be careful not to attach your love to things.

> # Love is for people, not stuff.

In the last chapter, you read about the physical side of clutter and how to deal with and prevent it (i.e. NEED vs. WANT). Your mental and emotional state plays a key role in both coping and prevention as well.

> # No matter how you slice it, how you *think* controls what you bring into your life.

Although using the logic vs. emotion approach is essential when it comes to letting go, it is perhaps even more critical when it comes to acquiring an item or taking on a new activity. The power of simplicity is most effective if you can prevent unneeded items from entering your life *in the first place*. How? By resisting the pull of IMPULSE.

IMPULSE

I
Must
Purchase
Until
Logic
Surpasses
Emotion

Impulse is pure emotion. If you apply logic to every "urge to acquire" that is based primarily on impulse, logic will win the battle almost every time. The challenge, of course, is to learn to use logic rather than emotion, to break the habit of instant gratification, and replace it with one of careful consideration.

Changing the soundtrack in your head is not an overnight process. You must make mental notes of how you currently think and give yourself the opportunity to develop alternative ways of framing the situation. You do this by using one of the most powerful, yet overlooked tools – the Power of Pause. Read on to learn more about this powerful tool.

REVIEW / EXERCISE

Do you operate from an emotional or logical standpoint?

_____

Are you content with your answer?_____

If not, what can you do to change your approach?

_____

_____

_____

What are some items that you have kept in your life because of your emotional attachment to them?

_____

_____

_____

_____

What are some items that you would like to eliminate from your life?

_____

_____

_____

_____

NOTES

_____

_____

_____

_____

CHAPTER 4

The power of pause

The investment of just a few minutes or seconds in a "pause" BEFORE anything new enters your life can make a monumental difference. The period of time before you decide to bring something new into your life can be the crucial "make or break point" in attaining simplicity. You have to make a *conscious* decision whether or not you have both physical and emotional room for it.

People often overlook, ignore, or just don't know about this important small space of time. You have to actually stop long enough to think about what you are doing. This escapes many of us because we run at such a fast pace that slowing down or stopping momentarily is a foreign concept.

However, the pause can be the defining moment in any situation, not just with simplicity. In any EVENT in your life, you have the opportunity to *choose* your REACTION, which will determine the OUTCOME.

EVENT + REACTION = OUTCOME

The Power of Pause is a free gift available to everyone. It usually occurs after an event and before your reaction.

For example, if you are on your way to work and someone pulls out in front of you (event), your initial reaction may be to blow your horn, add a few hand gestures, and top it all off with a smattering of name-calling that would put a truck driver to shame (reaction). This all occurs within seconds, perhaps within a split-second. All of this puts you in a nasty mood (outcome). You are so preoccupied with your anger that you miss your exit and arrive at the office late. You rush past the receptionist without saying hello. You get a call from your daughter and bite her head off when she asks you a simple question. People avoid you all day because of your foul mood.

The outcome of your day is determined just because of how you reacted to a simple event.

What if you had held off that initial reaction and instead chose to pause and think about what was happening? Your actions may have come out vastly different.

After you were cut off (event), you might think (pause), "This person is clearly in a hurry and I would be better off with him in front of me where I can keep an eye on him." OR "I hope I will still be driving when I am his age". You wave at him to let him know you see him (reaction). You proceed to arrive at work on time, warmly greet the receptionist, take your daughter's call and make arrangements to take her to dinner that night, and engage in several pleasant conversations with your coworkers throughout the day (outcome).

What a difference a PAUSE makes! Carrying that bad mood with you all day is anything but simple. It's heavy and tiresome, not only for you, but also for those around you.

The **real** formula should be:

EVENT + PAUSE + REACTION = OUTCOME

There is no doubt about it—you have to work at simplicity. Life will always go on around you, but only you are responsible and accountable for the choices that you make on a daily basis. Taking a moment to pause and consider your options is powerful. It can do many things:

- ❏ Alter your mood
- ❏ Affect others' moods
- ❏ Determine how people perceive you
- ❏ Impact the level of respect you receive
- ❏ Be the deciding factor in a promotion
- ❏ Set an example
- ❏ Influence your leadership skills

In other words, the PAUSE is powerful stuff!

So what's in a PAUSE?

The strategy of a PAUSE

Purpose
Assess
Understand
Stabilize
Execute

Purpose

First and foremost, you need to identify your *purpose* in life so you can determine whether something new "fits" into it according to your goals or objectives. If it doesn't fit, the process can stop here. If it does fit your purpose, you can proceed.

Assess

Look around at your office, your home, your emotional state, your schedule, and any area of your life that will be impacted by the new item. As you *assess* the situation and find that the effect is not acceptable, stop here. If it is acceptable, proceed.

Understand

As you assess what you are considering bringing into your life, you must *understand* the ramifications (both positive and negative) of how this will shape your life. If you can live with the consequences, proceed. If not, stop here.

Stabilize

By stopping, looking around, and being sure that you recognize the impact of your decision, you can alleviate any doubt that what you are planning to do is the best option. This is where you take your pulse to be sure that you are not racing to any snap decisions, but instead are on a steady path to a great decision. If the path is rocky, you may want to stop here. If you feel you have *stabilized*, move on.

Execute

If you made it this far, you can *execute* the plan knowing you have consciously decided what to do without any doubt that you are acting in the best interest of all involved. What a great feeling!

The Power of Pause is all about making thoughtful decisions, not impulsive decisions. That tiny investment of time can help you to reap huge rewards!

REVIEW / EXERCISE

EVENT + PAUSE + REACTION = OUTCOME

Purpose
Assess
Understand
Stabilize
Execute

Do you find yourself pausing before you make decisions?

_____

Is this an area in which you would like to see some improvement?

_____

How can you improve your decision-making ability?

_____

_____

_____

_____

_____

NOTES

_____

_____

_____

_____

_____

_____

_____

CHAPTER 5

Taking inventory

What do you love in your life? What don't you love in your life? If you say, "BUT I LOVE ALL MY STUFF!" you may have hit upon the core problem. If you love all of your stuff, you may be suffering from emotional thinking without pausing—a toxic combination when it comes to simplicity.

Literally taking an inventory of what you have in your life will be a productive step for you. Since clutter is what you no longer see, many times you don't even know what you have!

EXERCISE

Grab a pen and take a look at your space (home, office, storage unit, shed, car, garage, or anywhere that you live and/or store things) and, on the lines provided on the next page, list all the physical items that you see. On the following three pages, list all of the mental, emotional, and time activities in your life.

Below is a list of items and activities commonly found in homes and lifestyles. On the list below, put a checkmark beside the items that add nothing positive to your life.

- ❏ TV
- ❏ News/Newspapers
- ❏ Magazines
- ❏ Journals
- ❏ Catalogs
- ❏ Books
- ❏ Junk Mail
- ❏ Video games
- ❏ Season tickets
- ❏ Radio news
- ❏ Talk radio
- ❏ The Internet
- ❏ Email
- ❏ Instant Messenger
- ❏ Spam
- ❏ Telephone
- ❏ Interruptions
- ❏ Visitors
- ❏ Voice mail
- ❏ Cell phone
- ❏ Text messaging
- ❏ Pager
- ❏ Committees
- ❏ Meetings
- ❏ Reports
- ❏ Parties
- ❏ Shopping

Physical items:

❑ _____
❑ _____
❑ _____
❑ _____
❑ _____
❑ _____
❑ _____
❑ _____
❑ _____
❑ _____
❑ _____
❑ _____
❑ _____
❑ _____
❑ _____
❑ _____
❑ _____
❑ _____
❑ _____
❑ _____
❑ _____
❑ _____
❑ _____
❑ _____
❑ _____

Mental & Emotional:

❏ Always worrying about things I have no control over
❏ Feeling negative about everything
❏ Constantly reviewing my to-do list in my head
❏ _____
❏ _____
❏ _____
❏ _____
❏ _____
❏ _____
❏ _____
❏ _____
❏ _____
❏ _____
❏ _____
❏ _____
❏ _____
❏ _____
❏ _____
❏ _____
❏ _____
❏ _____
❏ _____
❏ _____
❏ _____

Time activities:

❑ ABC Board Meetings
❑ Carpooling kids
❑ Email
❑ _____
❑ _____
❑ _____
❑ _____
❑ _____
❑ _____
❑ _____
❑ _____
❑ _____
❑ _____
❑ _____
❑ _____
❑ _____
❑ _____
❑ _____
❑ _____
❑ _____
❑ _____
❑ _____
❑ _____
❑ _____
❑ _____

Miscellaneous clutter in your life

❏ _____
❏ _____
❏ _____
❏ _____
❏ _____
❏ _____
❏ _____
❏ _____
❏ _____
❏ _____
❏ _____
❏ _____
❏ _____
❏ _____
❏ _____
❏ _____
❏ _____
❏ _____
❏ _____
❏ _____
❏ _____
❏ _____
❏ _____
❏ _____
❏ _____

What can you eliminate?

Seeing your inventory on paper may surprise you with what fills your life. This inventory should not only open your eyes, but also provide the impetus to reassess and eliminate the items that are clogging up your life. My guess is that you could eliminate at least half of the items on these lists and still have plenty to keep you occupied and happy.

Here is an effective litmus test you can use when you consider eliminating time-consuming obligations, meetings, and activities. Every time you leave a meeting or finish an activity, ask yourself, "Do I feel the same as or better than when I arrived?" If you see a pattern with certain activities that you don't feel the same or better, you probably want to consider abandoning that activity. Don't judge it after just one bad experience, but if you have a series of bad experiences, that should send up a red flag.

CHALLENGE

Give yourself at least an hour of quiet time to sit down and study your lists. Contemplate what you can eliminate without feeling bad about it. Then choose a percentage (25%, 50%) of additional items that you would be willing to let go, regardless of how it makes you feel.

As you go through this process, run each item through the filters and employ the tools that you have already learned such as:

> NEED vs. WANT
> Logic vs. Emotion
> Create a new soundtrack
> Power of Pause

Letting go is difficult at first, but try your hand at it. Give yourself time to digest what life might be like without certain elements weighing you down.

Here are a few questions that may help you get started in the letting go process.

1. _____How many hours of television do you watch each week?

2. _____Could you cut that time in half?

3. _____Could you tape some of your favorite shows so you can watch them at your convenience and fast-forward through the commercials to save time?

4. _____Could you call the catalog companies and request to be taken off of their mailing list?

5. _____Could you drive your car without the radio on?

6. _____Could you limit the number of hours you work on your computer?

7. _____Could you turn your cell phone off?

8. _____Do you really want to serve on that committee?

9. _____Does your book club, bowling league, etc. refresh and energize you or weigh you down?

10. _____Are your social activities more habit than pleasure?

11. _____Are your children's lives truly enriched by each of their extracurricular activities?

12. _____Could you say "no" to going to or throwing parties?

These questions will blow some people's minds. Maybe options like these have never existed in your mindset before, but that is what makes this exercise so important.

Even though you may spend an hour or more on this exercise, consider it a long pause that will allow other alternatives to surface.

Continue this exercise until you have eliminated enough to make you feel a little uncomfortable. After all, there is merit in the cliché, "No pain, no gain." Revisit your list each week to keep it updated with eliminations and new additions.

This inventory will play a big part in your purpose and vision in life when you set goals. As we proceed, you will see that what you *have* is the foundation for what you *are*.

REVIEW/EXERCISE

What do you love in your life?

_____

_____

_____

_____

What don't you love in your life?

_____

_____

_____

_____

What can you eliminate?

_____

_____

_____

_____

NOTES

_____

_____

_____

_____

_____

_____

CHAPTER 6

See it, say it, believe it...
And it will come

Visualize whirled peas

(HINT: Read that out loud and it will make sense)

At birth, you were given two very important tools: visualization and self-talk. These are powerful natural partners, which means that you have to be careful with how you use them. The saying "Be careful what you wish for, you just might get it" is indicative of the power of visualization and self-talk.

I don't know about you, but the moment I decide to "see" something in my mind's eye, it happens. This can produce both positive and negative outcomes to any situation. If I am golfing and I visualize my golf ball being consumed by the water between me and the green, nine out of ten times, that ball will find its way into the water. But, if I walk up to the same shot and only "see" the green where the ball will bounce once then roll towards the pin, the same "rule" applies. I don't allow my mind's eye to "see" the water as an option.

You become what you think. You actualize what you believe. Your brain doesn't know truth from fiction, so it believes everything that you tell it. If you always say, "I am sick and tired of...", my guess is that you are often sick and feel very tired.

Because visualization works, you have to be careful what you wish for or think about. If you think big, you get big! If you think garbage, you get garbage. If you don't want much, you won't get much. If you think positive, you get positive. It's that simple.

Seeing something is one way to communicate to your brain through your mind's eye. But saying it to yourself or out loud can seal the deal. This is called self-talk. Some self-talk is oral (as when people say, "I'm just talking to myself"). Other self-talk is just that: talking inside yourself. No matter how hard you try, you can't silence the voice that is constantly chattering in your head. Unless you meditate or fall asleep, it is virtually impossible to quiet that voice. You may not always hear it, but rest assured that it is hard at work and can do severe damage to your psyche if left unchecked or ignored.

That's why it is so important to have goals that you can visualize and to affirm them with self-talk. Without goals, you are basically working without a plan or direction. Only about three percent of the world's population actually takes the time to write down their goals. They happen to be the most happy, healthy, and successful people on the planet. Not hard to believe that so few people set goals since we live in a world of instant gratification where we often have ideas and visions but lack the patience or energy to attain them, take the time to write them down, or explore what they mean. Goals are not *instant*, but rather ongoing. They can be short- or long-term in nature.

By setting goals, your thoughts and actions will naturally gravitate towards what you want. This is especially true when you *write down* your goals. It's one thing to think about your goals (which at that point are just dreams), and another thing to write them down. When you write down your goals, it is almost as if they are magnetic and your mind and actions are drawn towards them. Your subconscious sets out to work on them without your knowledge. Remember, your brain believes whatever you tell it and goes to work right away.

Setting goals will help you to develop a better sense of commitment and purpose in your life. You will set up realistic expectations that have meaning to which you can hold yourself accountable. If you take the time to set goals in writing, you will see them come to fruition.

GOAL SETTING AND SIMPLICITY

What do goals have to do with simplicity? By setting goals, you eliminate all the random clutter in your life on which you are currently wasting your time. You will start to let only things that you love into your life, and this will help you reach your goals. Goal setting is an important part of simplicity because it creates a standard or benchmark against which you measure all of your decisions.

Here's how it breaks down: Your purpose determines your vision. Your vision determines your goals. Your goals determine your tasks. And your tasks achieve your goals, vision, and purpose!

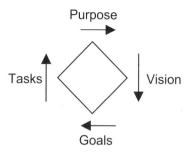

Purpose

Tasks

Vision

Goals

PURPOSE

What is your purpose? What is your life all about? What matters most to you? Is it family, career, money? If you are not quite sure how to answer that question, I suggest that you write your eulogy (ooh!). In other words, what do you want people to say about you when you are no longer of this world?

Not too long ago, traditional roles and purposes were clear-cut. The male went to work to earn money to raise his family; the female stayed home and raised the children.

Times have changed. I know that parents will always love their children, but the family unit has taken on a different shape. It seems that family doesn't have the same purpose any more. Parents now seem to focus on having a career and a bigger home, and giving their kids what they didn't have as children.

This is not right or wrong; it's just how things are. In this era, simplicity is more difficult to achieve than ever.

VISION

When you've defined your purpose, you can then move on to your vision. Your vision is how you see yourself fulfilling or carrying out your purpose. For example, if your purpose is to care for your family, your vision may be to encourage others to make their families the number one priority in their lives. A vision statement always starts with "I am." For example, "I am a great parent."

THE PAUSE THAT REFOCUSES

Harold Taylor of "Taylor's Time Tips" states, "a pigeon's eyes can't focus as it moves, accounting for it's strange walk. The bird has to pause between steps in order to refocus. It reminds me that we should frequently pause to refocus as well. If we proceed at a frantic pace without pausing, we could easily lose sight of our vision. Periodically review your goals and make sure your motion is moving you towards your vision."

GOALS

Starting out on a path without knowing where it leads is adventuresome. But do you really want finding your car keys to be an adventure every day? Goal setting may seem trite, but it is VITAL for success in any capacity of life, including simplicity. You need a picture in your mind of your desired results so you can start on the right path and know when you end up in the right place.

Know what you want and go after it. Once you know what you want, you can be discriminating and only allow those things into your life that will contribute to your success. One of the aspects of goal setting is writing down the benefits of the goals and why you want to achieve each goal. For example, if your goal is to simplify your life (and I hope it is!), you can review that goal's benefits when you try to find or use something that you got rid of. Then you will remember why you let it go in the first place and be content with your decision.

Any goal that you set should have these five characteristics:

S = Specific
M = Measurable
A = Achievable
R = Realistic
T = Time related

If your goals are not S.M.A.R.T., they aren't complete and may go unaccomplished. For example, the goal "to be rich" is too vague. But if you write down that you want to earn $80,000 by the last day of the current year, it begins to fit the S.M.A.R.T. model. It's Specific and Measurable ($80,000), and it is Time related (by the last day of the current year). Whether it is Achievable and Realistic, only you would know.

TASKS

By breaking down the steps needed to achieve each goal, you have just succeeded in creating your task list. Give each task a target date or deadline for completion.

At the end of this chapter, there is a set of goal setting worksheets. Take at least an hour of your time to discover your purpose, create a vision of what you want to accomplish, set goals that will help you achieve that vision, and prepare a list of tasks or steps that you need to take in order to meet your goals.

WORK BACKWARDS – START WITH THE END IN MIND

Having trouble getting started? Imagine that it is a year from today and write yourself a letter describing what you have accomplished in the past year and how you did it. Think about what you want your overall achievements to be for the next year, five years, or even your lifetime. In other words, see what you want and work backwards to see how you got there!

SHARE YOUR VISION

Don't keep your goals a secret. Share them with the important people in your life so that they can keep you on track and hold you accountable. Finding someone else that believes in setting goals and talking with them at least once a month is a great way to stay focused and make goal setting both fun and effective.

Let's look at how to set goals and follow through on them. Here's a sample of the process of goal setting.

Purpose

My purpose is to be a good example to my children and to teach them the skills needed to succeed in life.

Vision

A positive and present tense statement; not a future tense statement

I am organized and a great example for my children.

Goals related to vision

BE S.M.A.R.T.

1. Starting Monday, I will sort papers one hour each day.

2. By the first of next month, I'll make files instead of piles.

3. Starting tomorrow, I will use a day planner.

Tasks related to goals

Tasks occur at a planned time and place; schedule them in your day planner.

Goal #1 from above

Starting Monday, I will sort papers for one hour each day.

TASKS:

- In day planner, schedule an hour of sorting each day.
- Come to work prepared to do this.

Goal #2 from above

By the first of next month, I'll make files instead of piles.

TASKS:
- Purchase file folders on way home from work Thursday
- Schedule a half-hour each day to go through and sort papers to make filing system

Goal #3 from above

Starting tomorrow, I will use a day planner.

TASKS:

- Buy a day planner tonight.
- Enter all appointments and all addresses into it by the end of this week.

REVIEW / EXERCISE

The following pages are designed to help you set your own goals.

In my life right now, what is giving me the *greatest* sense of accomplishment?

_____

_____

_____

In my life right now, what is giving me the *least* sense of accomplishment?

_____

_____

_____

My personal strengths are:

_____

_____

_____

My purpose is:

_____

_____

_____

My vision is:

_____

_____

_____

_____

CATEGORIZE YOUR GOALS

Your life has many facets. Below are several areas in which you will want to set goals. Rank each category in order of priority. If you don't have a goal for a category, skip it and revisit it later to see if your direction has changed. You can have as many goals in each category as you want. Make a copy of this page if you need more room.

_____BUSINESS GOAL

_____

_____

_____

_____PERSONAL GOAL

_____

_____

_____

_____FINANCIAL GOAL

_____

_____

_____

_____FAMILY GOAL

_____

_____

_____

_____MENTAL GOAL

_____

_____

_____

_____SOCIAL GOAL

_____

_____

_____

_____SPIRITUAL GOAL

_____

_____

_____

_____PHYSICAL GOAL

_____

_____

_____

_____LEISURE GOAL

_____

_____

_____

_____COMMUNITY GOAL

_____

_____

_____

Your goal becomes more firmly planted in your head each time you write it down. That's why it is important to copy each goal to the first line of the following form. You should then break down each goal into the benefits, tasks, target dates, possible obstacles and solutions to overcome those obstacles, as well as affirmations to support your goal. You will want to make copies of the following form for each goal that you want to break down.

My goal is:

_____

_____

Benefits of achieving this goal are:

_____

_____

TASKS TO ACHIEVE THIS GOAL: (Schedule in day planner!)	Target Date	End Date
1._____		
2. _____		
3. _____		
4. _____		
5._____		

Possible Obstacles: Solutions:

_____|_____

_____|_____

_____|_____

Affirmations to support this goal:

_____

_____

_____

_____

_____

_____

_____

Take a moment to identify the possible obstacles and discover solutions that you may have otherwise ignored. Discuss these obstacles with someone else to generate even more ideas.

Affirmations to support your goal are statements that you can repeat to yourself throughout the day to further imbed the desired outcome into your head. This becomes a great part of your self-talk. Affirmations are always in the present tense and positive in nature. Some examples are:

- ❏ I am healthy.
- ❏ I am happy.
- ❏ I am organized.
- ❏ I am able to say no.
- ❏ I am a big-time winner!
- ❏ I am an important person.
- ❏ I feel totally great.
- ❏ My life is simple.
- ❏ I am one terrific person.
- ❏ I am prosperous now.
- ❏ People love to be with me.
- ❏ Money comes to me freely.

Make your own list of affirmations and write them on an index card to take with you wherever you go. Put one in your car, one in your purse or briefcase, and tape them onto your bathroom mirror. Be sure to say them out loud at least five times a day. Remember, your mind believes whatever you tell it!

MY DAILY AFFIRMATIONS

_____

_____

_____

_____

CHAPTER 7

Dealing with procrastination...NOW!

Procrastination:
The art of putting off until
tomorrow what can be done today.

Time clutter often comes in the form of having too much to do and no time to do it. It can also be as big a source of stress and anxiety as physical and emotional clutter. Procrastination is a key contributor to this problem and has caused many people to lose sleep, money, happiness, and probably years from their lives. Procrastination can inflict worry, stress, and fear that can be ignited just from the knowledge that you will have to finish doing things at the last minute.

The big question is why do we procrastinate? The answer can be simple: It's easier *not* to do the task because you don't like to do it. Or it can be more complex: Rather than allowing yourself to feel overwhelmed, you intentionally avoid thinking about the task until the last minute.

I don't claim to be a psychologist, so let's look at some simplistic and practical ways of handling procrastination. Here are four obstacles and solutions surrounding procrastination.

It is easier NOT to do something than it is to do it.

If you like to make to-do lists (either in your head or on paper), you may look up and down your list and gravitate towards the easier, lower priority tasks. It's easy to scan right over the less-than-attractive important tasks.

Solution

Schedule *all* of your to-do items in specific time slots in your day planner. You will check off a much higher percentage of tasks at the end of the day by doing this.

You put off the things that you don't like to do, aren't good at, don't really know how to do, or that seem unimportant to you.

Simply put, this is human nature.

Solution

If you find yourself pushing a task forward day after day, confront it. Ask yourself if there is someone else that could or would do it for you. If it is something that you just aren't good at, maybe you should consider educating yourself in that area so the task seems less daunting. For example, if you avoid turning in an expense report each month, find someone who loves math and ask if he or she will do the report for you. In return, offer to do something that you are good at for them. Or ask others how they do their reports— there might be a better or easier way of which you are unaware.

The task or project seems SOOOO overwhelming.

You have a huge project that is going to take 30 hours to do and you have six months to do it. That sixth month is here before you know it and you are scrambling to get it all done. This is *not* healthy.

Solution

Don't look at the task as a 30-hour project; look at it as six 5-hour projects. That means you only have to work on it for five hours per month over the next six months! That is much more do-able. Go even further by breaking the five-hours per month into five 1-hour projects (one hour per week) and scheduling each one-hour chunk into a time slot in your day planner. Doesn't that project seem much more manageable now?

You don't know where to start.

Finding a starting point can be tricky.

Solution

A great first step is to break down the project into small pieces. Decide what needs to be done to complete the project. By doing this, you will usually discover that the project isn't nearly as overwhelming or difficult as you first thought. After you list all of the steps, schedule them in your day planner. For example, if you want to organize your whole office (very overwhelming), start by narrowing it down to your desk (still too big), and then a specific drawer (manageable). That will get you started and you can then move on to the next drawer, then to the top of the desk, and so on in small steps.

You may be saying, "But I work best under pressure. I love to make a deadline and to feel that rush of adrenaline that I get when I'm under the gun." That may be true, but it could be because you have never tried to do something ahead of time to compare how you feel without that rush.

You have probably developed a habit of waiting until the last minute without even knowing it. To see if you are ready to break your habit and enforce your power of simplicity, try to work on a task by breaking it down into manageable bites and scheduling them far in advance so you can enjoy the freedom from worry. I think you'll like it!

REVIEW / EXERCISE

Procrastination: The art of putting off until tomorrow what can be done today.

To avoid procrastination:

Schedule *all* of your to-do items in specific time slots in your day planner.

If you find yourself pushing a task forward day after day, confront it.

Don't look at the task as a 30-hour project; look at it as six 5-hour projects.

A great first step is to break down the project into small pieces.

NOTES

_____

_____

_____

_____

_____

_____

_____

_____

_____

_____

_____

_____

CHAPTER 8

Take time to make time

Do you feel as if you are always short on time? If so, it may make you feel better to know that, sadly enough, many people regularly feel overwhelmed and rushed for time. An effective way to gauge just how overloaded you are is to examine what you find yourself doing in the car while driving.

Heaven forbid that we ever step into our vehicle to simply drive somewhere. How silly would that be? After all, aren't cars made for multitasking? Actually, they are. Just visit a car dealership or catch an auto show when manufacturers roll out their new models. You will see that they design their automobiles to accommodate today's busy lifestyle with CD and DVD players, cup holders, cell phone chargers, and VCR's.

According to a study done by AAA (the auto club) and researchers at the University of North Carolina, drivers are distracted 16.1 percent of the time that their vehicles are moving. The AAA Foundation for Traffic Safety reported that 71.4 percent of the drivers in a study were either eating or drinking while driving. Over 45 percent were grooming, 40 percent were reading or writing, and 34 percent were talking on a cell phone. (Source: *Toronto Star*, August 7, 2003.) And according to the book, *Road Rage to Road-Wise* by John Larson, driver inattention is the number one cause of traffic accidents. Multitasking while driving is a costly way to save time.

Do you find yourself doing any of these "other" tasks *while* driving?

❑ Eating
❑ Drinking
❑ Using your cell phone
❑ Putting on makeup
❑ Shaving
❑ Changing the radio station
❑ Changing tapes/CD's
❑ Taking care of the kids
❑ Putting a new disc in the DVD player
❑ Talking to passengers
❑ Reading
❑ Writing
❑ Reaching for something on the floor

What does this kind of multitasking get you? Not only is it dangerous, but it is proof that we don't have enough time to do some of these things when they should be done!

While the point of the study was to show the danger in driving while distracted, it also illustrates that we are so busy that we must multitask while driving. We have to perform certain chores and responsibilities while on the run, placing others and ourselves in danger.

Take a minute to reflect on a typical day in your life. How often do you come to the end of your day and wonder exactly what you accomplished? You ran all day, never took a break, skipped lunch, and you still feel as though you completed nothing of value. How frustrating! If you have more of these kinds of days than relaxing, fulfilling days, you may want to consider some methods for taking time to make time.

How do you make time? The first step is to become aware of the need to improve your performance and to find ways of working more effectively and efficiently. This alone can help you to simplify your life just by helping you to pay attention to how you perform certain tasks. From there, you can brainstorm ways to create shortcuts or cut steps out of the process.

Let's look at an example.

Say you have accumulated so much "stuff" in your life that you are almost paralyzed by it. Because of the amount of clutter, you don't know where to start to dig out. Perhaps you think it is a huge waste of time to declutter your life because it seems non-productive and has never worked in the past.

Instead of learning how to effectively begin the process and making a few habit adjustments, you decide that routinely searching for your glasses, keys, files, papers, cell phone, and scissors is easier. This way of thinking is completely counterproductive.

Consider investing the time in taking a class, reading a book, or hiring a professional organizer to learn how to successfully simplify, organize, and declutter your life. That investment will seem like a pittance of time compared to the time you save in the long run. Devoting a small portion of time can yield huge returns in the end.

After you become aware of the need to improve your performance and to find ways of working smarter, not harder, the next logical step is to analyze your time management skills.

If you run through your day and get nothing done, then this is the perfect time to *invest* an hour or two to look closely at how your days break down (both literally and figuratively).

Time management is such a basic skill that it is often overlooked. Don't let your eyes glaze over as you read this. Many of the most fundamental truths in life are basic, but we are so busy trying to keep up or get to the next level that the basics are often left behind in the dust.

If you let the emergencies of others run your day, you will wonder why you completed nothing that you set out to do. Here are some guidelines for taking time to make your time more effective.

1. Find a calendar that reflects how you see time (day, week, or month at a glance). If you have a drawer full of unused planners, it is likely that they don't look and feel right to you. For example, if you need to see the whole month at once and the planner is a day at a glance, you will not use it. Think about how you "see" time and purchase the proper planner. If you use an electronic day planner, you can toggle from one view to another…it's a beautiful thing. Your preferences may change as your lifestyle changes, so reevaluate yearly to see if your planner is still reflective and effective.

2. Take just ten minutes to plan your day. For every minute that you spend planning, you can save up to twelve minutes simply because you have a task to return to once you are done with an interruption. Scheduling just ten minutes in the morning or evening to plan for the day or the next day can save you up to two hours per

day! With a plan, you are more focused on what you need to accomplish. You'll see a big difference in what you are able to complete.

3. Try to schedule your day around your "prime time." Prime time is the time of day that you are at your best. Are you a morning person? Afternoon? Evening? Like to burn the midnight oil? You may even have more than one prime time throughout the day. Take that into serious consideration as you plan your day.

    Once you recognize your prime time, use it to your advantage. Schedule detail-oriented tasks when you are in peak form. Your concentration level is much more fine-tuned and mistakes are less likely during this time. Some examples of prime time tasks are reading detailed information, working on a proposal, writing an article, and calculating your taxes. Schedule mundane, repetitive tasks when you are not in your "zone." A high level of concentration isn't as necessary because these tasks can be done without much thought. This might include answering your email, paying bills, and returning phone calls.

    Once you know your prime time, try to learn the prime time of those around you. You can learn to work together more effectively by not interrupting each other's prime time. Productivity will increase and you'll have a better understanding of others' habits.

4. Have a to-do list, but take it another step further to simplify your time. Assign each task from your to-do list a time slot in your day planner to keep interruptions from usurping your whole day. That way, if someone says, "Can you finish this report?" you can look at your planner and say, "I can't do it right now, but I have time at 3:00 today. Will that work for you?" By popping tasks into time slots, you'll start to think more about how you can control your day.

5. Ask what NOW means. If your boss asks you to do something for her NOW and you typically drop everything else right away, back up a step. Make it a point to politely ask what NOW means. Often, she will say it is not needed until Friday or next week, but if you don't ask, you'll never know! So before you drop everything, be sure that you really have to.

6. Plan only 70-80 percent of your day to allow for flexibility, interruptions, and unplanned events. You want to be realistic, knowing that you are not going to have an interruption-free day. If you "plan" for emergencies and interruptions, you can easily shift and shuffle your plan around based on priority.

7. Don't procrastinate...just break the project down into "bite size" pieces and schedule the little pieces long before they are due. See Chapter 7 for more solutions to procrastination.

8. Prioritize your daily tasks. If someone is delegating to you and you don't know what is most important, you may be putting emphasis on tasks that are unimportant and non-urgent. Don't be afraid to ask what the top priority is. It is much easier to work with clarity than to beg forgiveness for doing the wrong thing first. Priorities may change throughout the course of a day, so don't hesitate to take a minute to review your planner and reprioritize as new projects arise.

9. Have only one calendar. This point is critical. You only have one life, so why would you need more than one calendar? You are only saddling yourself with more to carry and creating the perfect environment to double book yourself. If you don't check both (or in some cases, all three or four) of your calendars, you may forget an appointment or schedule more than one for the same time. The only exception to this rule is a family calendar on the refrigerator or in a location that everyone checks daily.

Effective time management can be the key to attaining simplicity. With a plan, you can do anything you set out to do!

REVIEW / EXERCISE

What do you find yourself doing while you are driving?

_____

_____

_____

How do you see time? A day, week, or month at a glance?

_____

_____

Guidelines for taking time to make your time more effective:

1. Find a calendar that reflects how you see time.

2. Take just ten minutes to plan your day.

3. Try to schedule your day around your "prime time."

4. Schedule your to-do list in time slots in your day planner.

5. Ask what NOW means before dropping everything.

6. Plan only 70-80 percent of your day to make room for flexibility, interruptions, and unplanned events.

7. Don't procrastinate...just break the project down into "bite size" pieces and schedule the little pieces long before they are due.

8. Prioritize your daily tasks.

9. Have only one calendar.

NOTES

_____

_____

_____

CHAPTER 9

So many choices... not enough time

You are now on a mission to simplify your life. Remember, simplicity does not mean that you have to sit back and wither away with nothing in your life but the air you breathe. In reality, you will always face daily situations that require willpower and thought, but you can set yourself up for success. You can limit the amount of exposure you have to unwanted stimuli and control how you react to that stimuli. In other words, if you usually shop excessively, stop going to the stores. Once you are at the store, you will need to employ the ideas in this chapter. There are a lot of choices to be made every day, so let's look at some of them.

Begin by imagining yourself going to the grocery store to buy a bag of potato chips. Remember when there were maybe ten choices of chips? Go to the store now and you are bombarded with *at least* 72 options of brands, flavors, packages, shapes, textures, styles, thickness, price, and size. What should be a simple snap-decision becomes a major decision-making process. It's a potato chip, for crying out loud! And heaven help you if you go to a SUPER sized grocery store where every chip under the sun is displayed. It could take weeks to get out of there if you take the time to consider all the choices presented to you.

Not only are the selections of product expansive, but so is the number of stores to choose from. If you go to the mall to buy a cell phone, you could be overwhelmed just trying to figure out where to go first.

You have a lot going on all day long when it comes to making decisions. You are confronted with:

- ❏ Work
- ❏ Family
- ❏ Friends
- ❏ School
- ❏ Laundry
- ❏ Sports
- ❏ Appointments
- ❏ Mail
- ❏ Bills
- ❏ Housework
- ❏ Taxes
- ❏ Email
- ❏ The Internet
- ❏ Church
- ❏ Social life
- ❏ Dinner
- ❏ Reading
- ❏ Shopping

The list could go on forever!

No matter what you want, it's out there in many ways, places, shapes, prices, and sizes. It is up to you to decide how much time you want to invest in any choice that you have to make. So how do you do that? Simple.

1. Be sure that you only spend a lot of time on important choices. If you find yourself spending an inordinate amount of time buying a pair of socks, you might want to settle for ones that are adequate rather than perfect.

Perfection:

Demand it of yourself and you'll always be unsatisfied.

Demand it of others and you'll always be disappointed.

Author Unknown

---

2. Limit the number of stores you will visit to track down an item. You can waste a lot of time and money searching for something that is only slightly different from the original one you found the week before in your search.

3. Allow yourself to accept "satisfactory." The best is actually not always worth the effort. If you go to buy a new computer and it only has *some* of the top of the line options, accept it, especially when you know that you will realistically never use even half of the options on the satisfactory computer.

4. Be content with what you have instead of discontent about what you don't have. Rather than constantly thinking about the one that "got away," be happy with the decisions you have already made. Nobody ever sets out

to make a bad decision, so you must have considered all the options at the time. Give yourself credit for having done that.

5. Don't listen to others. The old saying that the grass is always greener on the other side is rarely true. Others may try to convince you that the car you just bought isn't as good as their car, but who cares? When you weigh the differences of any choice you make, there is usually little difference. If you feel the need, explain to others why you bought your car, but don't make it a contest.

CHOICE

Contemplate
Having
Only
If
Considered
Essential

Let's take a look at how you can make better choices in a few of the many areas of your life, including:

- Shopping
- Technology
- Interruptions
- Life Balance
- Food and Eating
- Kids

- Television
- Sleep
- Financial
- Clothing
- Forgiveness
- Holidays

SHOPPING CHOICES

When it comes to shopping, you have plenty of choices, especially if you live in the city or suburbs. Not only do you have brick and mortar stores, but now you also have the Internet.

If you find that you do an extraordinary amount of impulse buying when you shop for commonly used items, the Internet can be a wonderful way to save money and time. Shopping online is an excellent option especially if you have the *"touching connection."* The touching connection happens when you hold an object in your hand and feel an emotional connection to it. If you saw an object from across the room, you would feel nothing. But the second you put your hands on it, you feel a bond. This is what makes online shopping such a great option—you can't touch anything!

WARNING: Be sure to set a timer or reminder on your computer to stop searching, or you may end up wasting valuable time and being counterproductive to your cause.

In order to limit the amount of shopping you do in stores, don't go to the stores. I know that may sound basic, but many of the most important truisms in life are basic common sense. Again, you want to set yourself up for success. Avoid the mall; instead, get a hobby (besides shopping), volunteer, learn a new craft, or discover your passion. Do whatever it takes to stay away from the stores.

Habitual or out of control shopping is not compatible with simplicity. Of course, we all have to shop at some point, but limit the temptations that may divert you from your mission of simplifying your life.

TECHNOLOGY CHOICES

Technology is expanding at breakneck speed, making it virtually impossible to be on the cutting edge. Before you bring home a new computer, digital recorder, MP3 player, cell phone, or even a television, they are practically obsolete.

For the pioneers of the world, not being on that cutting edge can be really irritating. If this sounds like you, it may be time to look around you and realize that most of the world is operating with older technology or none at all (GASP!).

Before you allow technology to rule your life, consider asking the following questions that relate to the NEED vs. WANT filter before you add anything new to your collection:

❑ Is what you have sufficient?

❑ Is what you are about to purchase going to make your life easier or more complicated?

❑ Can you live without it?

❑ Do you really **need** it or do you just **want** it?

❑ Is there a way to accomplish the same results without technology?

❑ Do you have room for this?

You shouldn't buy new technology just because you can.

> ## Purchase with purpose.

Take control of your technology before it controls you.

INTERRUPTION CHOICES

Maybe you have trained yourself to respond to interruptions as Pavlov's dog responded to the sound of a bell. Perhaps you have never thought about it, but you have the choice to respond to interruptions when and if you want to respond. Isn't that amazing?

To counter some of your reflexes or habits, try some of these techniques as they correspond to the potential interruptions below. If you answer "yes" to any of the following questions, the good news is that you can change your behavior.

1. If the phone rings, do you HAVE to answer it?

    Let the phone ring. At the very least, get and use caller ID so you can decide *before* you answer whether or not you want to talk to that person. Sometimes it is appropriate to turn off the ringer. Allow the call to go into voicemail or your answering machine and you can return the call when YOU are ready to talk.

2. When the doorbell rings, do you HAVE to open the door?

    Get a peephole in your door so you can decide if you should answer it. This is also a good safety tip.

3. When you hear the sound of a new email arriving, do you have to read it?

    In order to avoid hearing or seeing the new email notification, close your email program. Only open it when you are scheduled to read and respond to email. If you can't close the program, at least turn off the notification so it doesn't distract you every time a new email arrives.

4. When you read an email, do you have to respond immediately?

    Just because you read an email does not mean that you have to answer it right away. Mark email that requires action or a reply from you as unread. Usually this means it will be in bold print so you know that you have to take care of it later on.

5. When someone says they need something done, do you assume it has to be done right away?

    As explained in Chapter 8, if someone comes to you in a panic that something needs to be done right away or NOW, always clarify what "right away" or "NOW" means. Most times, it means that day or week. It doesn't always mean this very instant. ASK! When people come to you with an "emergency" project or task, their goal is usually to get it off of their desk and onto yours.

6. When a visitor comes into your home or office, do you have to spend time with them?

    Getting rid of an unannounced guest can be difficult. Try standing up when someone walks in or drops by; it is usually more uncomfortable to stand and have a conversation. If they don't get the hint, start to walk towards the door. If that doesn't work, tell them that you have to go to the restroom (I hope they won't follow you) or that you have to finish the project you were working on when they came in. If you have comfortable chairs in your office, consider getting rid of them or putting them farther from your desk so a normal conversation is harder to achieve.

    Another obvious tactic is to be honest. Tell the person that now is really not a good time and you would love to visit but you have a deadline. Put yourself in the visitor's shoes and realize that most people appreciate the truth.

7. When the mail carrier arrives, do you have to get and open the mail?

    For simplicity's sake, open your mail daily. This does not mean you should allow your mail carrier to interrupt your day to hand you the mail. Retrieve the mail when you are ready to open and process it. Dare to be boring and open it at the same time and place every day. Always open your mail over a trashcan since at least 50 percent of your mail is junk and envelopes.

Be more aware of your surroundings and the patterns in your day as they relate to interruptions. It's usually not the actual interruption that complicates your life and makes you feel as if you've accomplished nothing; what drains you is the instant cut-off of energy when you stop doing a task and the ramping back up to resume the task. That is why it is better to continue with the task at hand before taking on a new one. This is not always possible, but if you learn to recognize your energy-drainers, you can begin to find ways to work around them.

Fewer interruptions means more simplistic living.

LIFE BALANCE CHOICES

Say it with me. "**NO**." Again. "**NO**." If you expect to find any sense of balance in your life, you need to practice saying **NO**. It could quite possibly be the most difficult little word in the world.

Before you consider taking on *any* new activity, you need to be crystal clear that there is room in your life for it *without* sacrificing what matters to you most. Too often, the word "yes" comes out before you realize the consequences.

Life balance relies heavily on all of the concepts that you have read about so far in this book, but especially on the Power of Pause. Without it, you keep adding more time-consuming activities without any thought to what will suffer.

Look at it this way. You only have 24 hours in a day, 168 hours in a week, 8760 hours in a year. How do you want to spend them? Do you like the way you are spending them now? How much quality time do you give to your children, spouse, friends, and others in your life? Ask yourself these important questions before you say **yes**.

How do you say no? Don't answer right away when you are asked to do something new. Say you will look into it, and then do a little homework. It might end up that you can politely say, "I don't think that I can serve on the board at this time, but I spoke with Mary and she is willing to offer her time and expertise." OR "I don't think I can serve at this time because, after careful consideration, I realized that I just don't have the time. I won't make a commitment that I can't fulfill. I'm sure you can understand."

Balance your life by simply saying, "No, thank you".

FOOD & EATING CHOICES

Eating is often done on the run at a hurry-up-and-get-it-done pace, as if eating were a chore. Therefore, we don't give much thought to *how much* we eat, let alone *what* we eat. Very often we may eat more than we need to satisfy our hunger (which, by the way, happens to be the main purpose of eating).

According to the media, we are on the verge of a serious health crisis in this country due to obesity. I am not a diet and exercise guru, but I am a choice guru. Yes, you have choices even when it comes to eating!

The food that you eat now may not even resemble food in its natural form, but manufacturers keep making our life *simpler* by producing easy-to-prepare-and-inhale meals. All of this is done in the spirit of saving us time, but it does nothing to save us money, calories, or fat. This is only one of many factors that have brought about this health epidemic.

Did you ever stop to think about the food you eat? Flash frozen, freeze-dried, dehydrated, vacuum-packed, canned, chemically preserved, powdered...all such *scrumptious* words when associated with food. When was the last time you made homemade bread?

I confess I occasionally like a greasy cheeseburger as much (or as little) as the next person, but frankly, some fast foods resemble manmade plastics. Sure they taste good (on a rare occasion), but what are they doing to your body? Eating on the run is normal now, but these poor eating habits are being passed on to children! In fact, fast food places gear their marketing towards children so they grow up on their food and continue on into adulthood not knowing that they have other choices.

What food are you putting in *your* body?

When making food choices, you most definitely want to use the Power of Pause. Think before you eat. You are in control of what you put on your table and into your body, but first you have to stop long enough to assess your current eating habits. From that assessment, you can set a course for your future food choices for you and your family.

If you *plan* your meals ahead of time instead of on the run, you can make a significant difference not only in your weight, but also in how you feel! Plus, there is another bonus when you plan your meals: You will spend less time and money in the grocery store because you will shop from a prepared list and less on impulse. Make a computerized checklist of commonly purchased items and keep copies in the kitchen so you can check off what needs replaced.

Investing some time in your body will provide a return almost immediately. Go back to the basics by covering the four food groups (sorry, chocolate is not a food group), stay aware of what you eat, and watch the energy in your life increase. You can eat a healthy diet without being extravagant.

But wait: With whom do you eat? When I was growing up, families always ate dinner together at the same time each night. Do you? Simplicity involves quality time with your family and with those about whom you care most. A family eating dinner together even three times a week is more the exception than the rule. What a shame. See if you can make time in your life to spend an hour around the table with the most important people in your life. After all, isn't family what life is all about?

If you are single and/or live far away from your family, you may want to tuck this information away or make an effort to spend meal time with people you care about. If you are a family in which the adults are forced to work on incompatible schedules, eating together may be something to strive towards in the future. Perhaps breakfast, lunch, or even a snack time together would make a difference.

KID'S CHOICES

You have a huge impact on how your children make choices when they are young; these habits will also carry on into adulthood. Kids emulate the way you make choices. If you don't limit them on their choices, they can wind up wanting everything. If they get used to this unlimited freedom, they will continue to expect no limitations as they grow up. By the time your child enters adulthood, he or she is not equipped to make good choices. So in reality, giving your children unlimited choice is doing them a disservice.

Let's talk about kids' toys. Take a moment and think back to your childhood. Did you have a plethora of toys to play with or did you have just a few? Did you have so many that you couldn't decide what to play with first? One of the biggest complaints I hear from my clients is that their homes have more toys than a toy store. My first question is, "Who buys those toys?" Usually it is the parents, with an occasional donation from the grandparents and other relatives. My second question asks how the parents can expect a child to decide what to play with when faced with so many options. Most of the toys go untouched, unappreciated, and are thrown into piles to be tripped over.

Someone once said that a form of child abuse is giving your children everything you didn't have. A child can become over-stimulated and burdened by the number of toys and activities that fill his or her life. Of course, children will continue to ask for new things because they receive them upon request. It is up to you as a parent to curb your "giving," especially if you are giving for the wrong reasons, such as out of guilt.

If grandparents and other family members are contributing to the problem, ask them instead to buy U.S. savings bonds, stocks, or gift certificates for consumable items such as movie passes, concert tickets, and restaurants. Explain to them that you are simplifying your family's life and would greatly appreciate their understanding and respect for this venture. If they refuse to participate, you can teach your children to let go of a toy each time they receive a new one (ONE IN-ONE OUT). Make it a family event to go to a children's shelter to donate the toys so your kids understand the art of giving.

Activities can also clutter your child's life. A child can play any sport under the sun, and those choices can be overwhelming. Most teams allow everyone to participate so there is no chance of not making the team. This can encourage involvement in simultaneous activities. Ballet, dance, karate, piano, drums, violin, and acting lessons are also available for consideration at the same time.

Help your children make thoughtful decisions about what they become involved in. Be sure to set a limit on the number of activities they are allowed to participate in concurrently. **One** is a good number to start with.

Remember when you used to go outside and play? That meant being creative by inventing games and playing some of the standard ones like hide and seek, kickball, baseball, football, dodge ball, red rover, catch, and running through a sprinkler.

Try to peel your children away from the television, video games, and computer long enough to go out and exercise and discover new styles of recreation. Don't let MTV raise your child.

Simplicity can be the best lifelong gift you give your children.

TELEVISION CHOICES

By age 65, most Americans have
watched more than 9 years of television!

From *Bayprint Impressions*, April 2002

If you are under 65, the number of years of television that
you will have watched by age 65 will be dramatically higher
than the statistic above. Imagine your children's exposure.
Today's five-year-olds may very well end up spending
decades of their life in front of a screen!

Television is amazing. How that picture shows up on my
screen is beyond me, but it does. Television can be
addictive, and if you are not careful, you could end up
spending more of your free time in front of the tube than
anywhere else. It has become a household staple,
remaining on 24/7 in some cases.

What is more amazing about television is the number of
channels from which to choose. And the *most* amazing part
is that, even with hundreds of channels, there is still often
nothing of value to watch.

This one piece of technology has kept us from lying in the
grass looking at the clouds, baking a homemade apple pie
(crust and all), or just sitting around with the whole family in
the evening getting to know one another better.

Watching TV is a time-consuming activity that takes place
almost unconsciously, and is transformed into a habit for
many somewhere along the way. Do you have a soundtrack
from your childhood that says the TV should be on all the

time? Are you creating that soundtrack for your children? Do your children have their own television in their room? Television can separate a family, making "a day in the life of simplicity" nearly impossible to achieve.

Entertainment is an important part of life, but there may be such a thing as too much of a good thing. You could end up spending a good portion of your life with one dimensional characters you will never meet while those you love go unattended.

Television and the media have created a society of information and news junkies. So many people I meet feel that they couldn't go through the day without their newspaper or television news. Why? If something happens in the world that you should know about, you will hear about it. You don't have to know everything.

And since when did the weather qualify as news? In my travels, I make it a point to watch local news (for research) and am always amazed that the weather is usually the first piece of news. Can't you get the same results by sticking your head out the door? There has been weather as far back as I can remember; it rained, it snowed, it was windy, it was sunny, and sometimes it sleeted or hailed. Weather is not exactly "news."

When making choices about television, there are several things to consider.

❏ The amount of time you want to spend watching

Track how much time you spend watching TV for one week. Ask yourself if you could do something more productive with that time. Imagine if you took only three or four hours of your TV time each week and spent it with your family. Turn TV time into quality time.

❏ The package that you have with your cable company or satellite provider

If you are constantly surfing the channels, you may have a package that offers too many choices. Consider dropping down to a lower package to avoid jumping around so much. And you'll save money, too.

❏ The content that you watch

As you track the amount of time that you watch TV, go one step further and also log *what* you watch. Review the content to see if it contributes to your well-being or detracts from your core values and hardens your sensitivity to life.

❏ The purpose of what you watch

Ask yourself why you watch television. Are you avoiding doing something more important? Do you just need to unwind? Do you like the entertainment value? Are you overly interested in a topic (such as weather)? Do you feel that you *have* to watch the news? Is there really no reason…you just watch out of habit?

❏ How watching TV affects you

Do you feel like a couch potato? Do you feel educated (learning about history)? Does TV make you think? Does it make you feel uneasy (violence)? Does it stretch your mind (legal strategies, mysteries)? Does TV make you feel better or worse? Could you live if you missed your favorite shows?

This exercise is not meant to make you defensive about the television that you watch, but to compel you to take a closer look at your viewing practices and patterns. You may have forgotten that you have choices to make in this area because you have been lulled into thoughtless routines. Pay attention to see if television is adding to or taking away from the quality of your life.

Don't want to give up TV? You don't have to. Simplify your life and save time all at once by using TiVo (check with your cable company or satellite provider) or programming your VCR to tape your favorite shows. (Yes, you can learn how to program your VCR.) When you watch what you've recorded, you can fast-forward through the commercials, saving time and money. (You'll save money because you won't see products that you don't need but feel compelled to buy.)

P.S. If you know you are an impulse buyer, avoid watching infomercials and shopping networks!

SLEEP CHOICES

So what does sleep have to do with simplicity? You may think that sleep is a waste of time, but without it, your clarity and focus are compromised, thus complicating your life. Inadequate sleep can be a huge time-waster. Lack of sleep reduces innovative thinking by 60 percent and flexibility in decision-making by 39 percent. (Source: *Organizational Behavior & Human Decision Processes*, 1999.)

Many people walk around as if they never sleep. The reason is…they don't…at least not as much as they should. Who has time to sleep?

Want to know the secret to getting more sleep? Schedule it.

Ever since I was very young, one thing that I have REFUSED to sacrifice, if at all possible, is my sleep. If I get less than seven hours or more than eight, I know that I am not someone that you want to contend with throughout the day. In fact, if I could get away from myself on those days, I would.

How many hours of sleep do you need? If you need seven or eight, going on four and five hours is tolerable for about one or two nights. If you do this repeatedly, your productivity and disposition are compromised. Oversleeping can have the same effect.

Do you go to bed too late and then hit the snooze button 14 times before you get up in the morning?   Do you fall asleep at work (or wish you could)? Are you always cranky? (Ask your family or co-workers!) Try going to bed earlier. The answers to these questions may give you some insight and spark you to review your sleep habits.

> # Habits are prime targets for choice and change.

Just because you are not a morning person does not give you the luxury of telling your boss that you can't make it to work by 8:00 a.m. If you do have that flexibility, I recommend using it. If not, go to bed earlier. And go to bed at the same time EVERY NIGHT so that waking up is not such a problem. By investing in a good night's sleep, you will be crisp and able to accomplish more during the day.

Remember your "prime time"? Think about the time of day when you are at your best. Seriously take that into consideration as you plan your day AND night!

Learn your prime time and concentrate on getting the proper amount of sleep for a week (that's not such a major commitment, is it?), and you will feel better and be more productive. (And those around you will be glad you did!)

A good night's sleep will remove the fuzziness that hinders your decision-making skills. In turn, this will positively add to your mission of simplicity.

FINANCIAL CHOICES

For most people, money and finances are more difficult to talk about than sex. Let the record reflect that I am neither a financial planner nor a sex therapist, but I am what you might call frugal (not to be confused with cheap).

How do you view money? Do you see it as something to spend? If so, read this carefully: Money is NOT to be spent; money is to be managed.

Financial woes are often the result of living beyond your means. In other words, you spend more than you make. Often, financial choices are based on the need for instant gratification, which really boils down to an impulse, not a conscious choice. Typically, there is little or no thought given to the future consequences of instant gratification, such as huge credit card balances and unsecured debt.

Sadly, retailers rely on this weakness. Rarely do we *have* to wait to buy anything since retailers are so accommodating with instant credit at zero percent interest for three years. The temptations are hard to resist, but you must.

Financial choices are prime candidates for the **NEED vs. WANT** filter. If you **"pause"** long enough to run financial decisions through this filter, you will soon realize that you don't really want all of the irritants that come with the purchase. Sure, buying new stuff is exciting and liberating; but then you have to live with it, maintain it, pay for it, and stress over it for the next decade. Is that what you really want?

Emotions play a key role in financial choices. Fear surfaces at the thought of missing out on a sale or letting a coupon expire. Competition flares when you compare your possessions with those of your family, friends, neighbors, or coworkers. Joy kicks in when you think of acquiring something new. Jealousy sparks when you see someone with something you wish you had. These are powerful emotions, to say the least.

Logic must be engaged when it comes to finances. You can't let your emotions run away with your money. If you do, you will soon find yourself deep in debt.

If you find yourself in debt and struggling with your financial choices on a daily basis, I have two words for you: Mary Hunt. Mary Hunt is the author of *Cheapskate Monthly*, a newsletter that provides hope, encouragement, inspiration, and motivation to individuals who are committed to financially responsible and debt-free living. It also provides the highest quality information and resources in a format exclusive of paid advertising. You will find the *Cheapskate Monthly* filled with tips, humor, and great information to help you stretch those dollars till they scream! Learn more by visiting www.cheapskatemonthly.com.

Financial freedom can be the cornerstone of simplifying your life. Without the burden of financial worries, you can soar!

CLOTHING CHOICES

You're probably wondering what in the world clothing has to do with simplicity. The fewer choices you have when getting dressed, the easier it is to decide what to wear.

Every day, you probably skim over the same clothes in your closet that *still* don't fit, are *still* uncomfortable, *still* need to be altered, *still* have a stain that won't come out, or are *still* out of style. Why not take the time to make choices about what you really want to keep and will realistically wear? Then donate the clothes you no longer need or want.

Where there are clothes, there is laundry. Don't like doing laundry? Try these tips.

❑   Do the laundry on the same day(s) each week.

This let's everyone know that they need to have their clothes in the hamper on the right day. It will help in planning what to wear as well. If you know you need your white blouse for Friday's meeting, you won't wear it on Tuesday if laundry day is Saturday.

❑   Consider using a laundry sorter.

Instead of one hamper that catches every piece of dirty laundry, try a laundry sorter. The triple compartment type allows you to pre-sort light, dark, and delicate clothing (or whatever your types are).

❑   Reuse bath towels.

This can seriously reduce the amount of laundry you do each week. You *are* clean when you come out of the shower, so how dirty is the towel? Be sure to let them hang to dry between showers.

❏ Realize that doing the laundry only takes a little time.

The washer and dryer are doing most of the work! While the washer is washing and the dryer is drying, you can relax and say, "I'm busy doing the laundry!"

❏ Eliminate the hanger tangle.

Take a few minutes to sort your hangers, throw away or recycle the ones you don't like, and consider buying a hanger organizer. Empty hangers take up space in your closet, so keep them cycling to the laundry area.

By reducing your wardrobe, paying more attention to your laundry, and only putting clothes in the laundry that are truly dirty, you can simplify your clothes and laundry life!

FORGIVENESS CHOICES

Do you hold grudges so long that you can't even remember what they're about? If you answered yes, it might be time to make some adjustments to how you handle difficulty and confrontation.

In order to use a well-rounded approach to simplifying your life, you must constantly pay attention to the internal elements of your life. Internalizing resentment, hatred, bitterness, animosity, and hostility is heavy business.

Get a piece of paper and a pen and jot down the areas of bitterness in your life. With whom are you angry? Why? When did the incident occur that caused this anger and resentment? What makes your blood boil and why?

Now take that piece of paper and crumple it up, tear it up, burn it in a fireplace, or perform a personal ceremony to eliminate that paper along with the anger from your life.

Forgiveness is a choice. Holding a grudge is a choice. Guess which one is easier to carry every day? Grudges weigh a ton. Not only do you have to carry the weight of the emotion, but you also have to remember why you are upset. That is a lot of work!

If you have road rage, be sure to employ the Power of Pause. Forgive someone as they cut you off. It has happened before and it will happen again. Move on.

Simplify your life and let go of the anger. Choose forgiveness.

HOLIDAY CHOICES

Ah, the holiday season…a time for joy and celebration. Or is it? Sometimes the holidays feel more like a lead blanket of stress than a carefree time of fun.

The problem is all the clutter! Not just the physical clutter, but also the mental, emotional, and time clutter that comes with the holiday season. The parties, the family get-togethers, the obligatory gift buying, the pressure to out-do the gift from the year before, the running around and standing in long lines to buy things that nobody really wants, the baking of holiday cookies, and everything that goes along with that time of year.

Make the holiday season a more meaningful, pleasant experience to look forward to rather than an ulcer-inducing occasion. You can simplify your holidays by using the following HOLIDAY SIMPLICITY ideas.

- Before you commit to any holiday activity, ask yourself, "If I *don't* do this, what will happen?" If the answer is something that you can live with, then don't do it! For example, if you've always gone to your aunt's house for your holiday dinner but you only do so out of tradition (or guilt), ask what would happen if you didn't go. If you won't be disowned, consider starting a new tradition of a quiet family dinner at your own home.

- Plan your holiday season. Limit yourself to a set number of parties (hosting and attending) to avoid over-commitment. As you plan, be sure to schedule only those things that will bring you joy.

- When it comes to decorating, don't just put it on your to-do list. Actually schedule a time to do it and involve the whole family to make it fun.

- Many container companies have made life much simpler by designing storage containers made especially for the holidays. They come in a variety of shapes, sizes, and colors that make identifying them easy and logical. (For example, there are color–coded containers with lids, and tube-shaped containers that easily accommodate rolls of wrapping paper.) This makes retrieving and storing items an effortless task rather than a time-consuming chore.

- Ask for and give gifts that take up no space, such as restaurant gift certificates, lottery tickets, spa or salon services, or movie passes. You can purchase them by phone or online, thus considerably reducing your shopping time (and avoiding impulse buying).

- Make a conscious effort to ignore all of the commercialism that the holidays produce and you may find yourself less inclined to participate in all the hype.

- If you have a holiday card list full of technology-savvy folks, consider sending e-cards instead of the usual snail mail. Only try this if it will not offend your mailing list.

Even though the holiday season is typically in November and December, remember that holidays are peppered throughout the year. Therefore, no matter what time of year you are reading this section, rest assured that a holiday will pop up before you know it. Simplifying your holidays can spread joy all year long!

REVIEW / EXERCISE

CHOICE

Contemplate
Having
Only
If
Considered
Essential

You have choices in many areas, including:

- ❏ Shopping
- ❏ Technology
- ❏ Interruptions
- ❏ Life Balance
- ❏ Food and Eating
- ❏ Kids

- ❏ Television
- ❏ Sleep
- ❏ Financial
- ❏ Clothing
- ❏ Forgiveness
- ❏ Holidays

Where can you make better choices?

_____

_____

_____

_____

_____

_____

_____

CHAPTER 10

Speaking simply...

So how do you proceed to simplicity? I hope that by now you are committed to the concept of simplifying your life.

You had a glimpse of "A day in the life of simplicity" in the beginning of this book. Take a moment and imagine yourself living the live that you want to live.

In order to unleash your power of simplicity, below are some action steps that you can take immediately to put you on the right path.

❑ If you haven't done so already, complete the goal setting exercise in Chapter 6. You need a definition of your future, and your goals will provide that definition.

❑ Speaking of definitions, you must first define what simplicity means to you, what it looks like, and the steps you can take to make that happen.

❑ Visualize your future the way you want it to look, and then what you see will be what you'll get. If you think small, you'll get small. Think big and you'll get big. Don't be afraid to think big.

❑ Start to live the life that you seek. Don't wait until you are "ready" to simplify and have the time to do so. You will never be ready or have the time until you make it a priority.

❑ Make time to be with the ones that you love. This is a giant component to achieving simplicity. The more time you spend with those that are important to you, the less important your old stresses become.

❑ Start spending time doing the things that you love. Evaluate what you are doing now and try to cut that list in half. Stop wasting time doing unnecessary tasks and instead make time for the things you love to do.

❑ Stop living in the past. Learn to forgive and try to forget. Yesterday is history; treat it as such. Live for today and plan for tomorrow.

❑ Assess your existing habits and consider new ways of doing things.

❑ Listen closely to your self-talk. What are you saying to yourself? Pay attention and change anything negative to something positive.

❑ Choose to let go of the small stuff; it only weighs you down.

❑ Get to know yourself better. Be more in tune with your thoughts and actions.

Simplicity is not easy, but you now have the essentials to successfully begin the process and achieve it.

Remember that simplicity is not an event. It is a lifestyle, a choice, <u>YOUR</u> choice, a journey, and an ongoing path.

I am genuinely passionate about serving you with the tools to recognize the need and motivation to achieve simplicity in your life. If you have a success story of transforming a complicated, unhappy life to a simplified existence (before, during, or after reading this book), I urge you to email your story to me at patty@ByeByeClutter.com.

What I wish for you is what I wish for myself…simplicity, on your own terms. If you choose to live your life on purpose, simplicity will follow.

The POWER OF SIMPLICITY is within you!

ABOUT THE AUTHOR

Patty Kreamer is the President of Kreamer Connect, Inc., a Pittsburgh-based company that helps individual and corporate clients become more productive and perform better while at the same time simplifying their work and lives. Sounds impossible? Not with Patty.

Author - Patty's first book "But I Might Need It Someday" helps individuals understand the habits that keep them from organizing their work and lives. Then, it shows them how to overcome their natural tendencies and conquer clutter, in all its forms, once and for all.

Speaker - Patty creates custom programs for regional and national corporate and association audiences on topics ranging from organizing workspaces to enhancing productivity to creating simplicity in chaotic lives.

Consultant - Patty works with corporate managers to help them identify gaps in productivity, streamline paper and processes, and help groups of people work better together.

Organizer - Patty helps people say good-bye to clutter in their homes and offices.

Patty is seen regularly in the media as she shares her frank, fun, and energetic style with the audiences of publications like The Pittsburgh Post Gazette, Pittsburgh Business Times, and through television shows like Age Wise, KDKA TV's Morning Show, and One on One with Lee Adams.

As founder of the Pittsburgh Professional Organizers, a qualified member of the National Speakers Association and a member of the National Association of Professional Organizers, Patty leads the way in spreading the word about how we can be more productive, perform better and simplify our lives.

Patty and her husband, George, live in a simplified and uncluttered home in Pittsburgh with their dog, Bear.